Sharen

INFORMATION LIBRARY

WEATHER AND CLIMATE

Theodore Rowland-Entwistle

Gareth Stevens Children's Books
MILWAUKEE

Library of Congress Cataloging-in-Publication Data

Rowland-Entwistle, Theodore.
 Weather and climate / Theodore Rowland-Entwistle ; [illustrated by Oxford Illustrators
Ltd. and Eugene Fleury]. — North American ed.
 p. cm. — (Gareth Stevens information library)
 Includes index.
 Summary: Introduces the elements that make up weather and climate, discusses
methods of gathering data and forecasting the weather, and examines the climate's
effects on animals and vegetation, and the effect of human activities on climate.
 ISBN 0-8368-0062-1
 1. Weather—Juvenile literature. 2. Climatology—Juvenile literature. [1. Weather. 2.
Climatology.] I. Fleury, Eugene, ill. II. Oxford Illustrators Ltd. III. Title. IV. Series.
QC981.3.R68 1991
551.5—dc20 90-24089

North American edition first published in 1992 by
Gareth Stevens Children's Books
1555 North RiverCenter Drive, Suite 201
Milwaukee, Wisconsin 53212, USA

Photographic credits: Heather Angel, 38 (right); Aquila, 41 (right); Biofoto, 4;
British Antarctic Survey, 57 (right); Canadian National, 15; John Cleare/
Mountain Camera, 29 (left), 32 (left and right); Crown copyright 17; Depart-
ment of Electrical Engineering, University of Dundee, 12; Patrick Eagar, 8; ET
Archive, 37; Sally and Richard Greenhill, 5 (bottom left); Susan Griggs/
Comstock, 30, 31; Robert Harding Picture Library, 38 (left), 41 (top), 42 (left), 45
(top and bottom), 47 (bottom right), 52; Eric and David Hosking, 41 (bottom
left); Hutchinson Library, 25, 39 (left), 51 (top), 53; G. V. Mackie, 16; Magnum,
39 (right), 42-43, 51 (bottom), 54, 58-59; S. & O. Mathews, 5 (top and center
right); NASA, 57 (left); Oxford Scientific Films, 17, 43 (right); Panos Pictures, 59
(right); Photo Library of Australia, 36; Science Photo Library, 21, 28, 29 (right),
33, 34, 35, Charles Tait, 47 (top); ZEFA, 23

Illustrated by: Oxford Illustrators Ltd. (Jonathan Soffe, Simon Lindo, and Ray
Webb) and Eugene Fleury

Series editors: Neil Champion and Rita Reitci
Research editor: Scott Enk
Educational consultant: Dr. Alistair Ross
Designed by: Groom and Pickerill
Picture research: Ann Usborne
Specialist consultant: Dick File

Contents

1: WEATHER OR CLIMATE?

What's the Difference?

Arctic Circle

Tropic of Cancer

The Equator

Tropic of Capricorn

Antarctic Circle

Those circles

The equator, the Arctic Circle, and the Antarctic Circle are imaginary lines on a map. At the equator, all the days are just as long as the nights.

The Tropic of Cancer marks the farthest north the Sun appears to travel during the northern summer (reached by June 21), and the Tropic of Capricorn marks the farthest south the Sun travels during the southern summer (reached by December 21).

The Arctic Circle marks the place where there is one winter day of the year when the Sun does not rise. The Antarctic Circle marks the same place for winter in the Southern Hemisphere. Traveling farther inside these circles means experiencing more sunless winter days and nightless summer days.

Weather and climate are two ways of looking at changes and variations in temperature, wind, rain, and sunshine. The word "weather" refers to all the day-to-day changes in any one place. Scientists who study weather are called meteorologists.

The word "climate" describes the usual weather found in any one place over many years. Scientists who study climate are called climatologists. Most experts regard 30 years as the time needed to know the climate of a place. But some scientists think 50 or even 100 years give a more accurate picture.

The climate varies from one place to another. We expect long, hot, sunny days in summer in California, but in Ontario the same summer may be hot or cold, dry or wet. So we say that California and Ontario have different climates.

Different climates

We find even bigger differences when we compare the climates of the tropics — the regions near either side of the equator — with the climates of northern Europe or northern North America. The tropics are hot all year round, with two main seasons — wet and dry. But the northern areas have four seasons — spring, summer, autumn, and winter.

Changes in climate

The various climates of the world have changed over the years. Only 20,000 years ago, ice covered large areas of Europe, Asia, and North America. The ice sheet reached as far south as the Great Lakes in North America and the Thames River in England.

Climates are still changing today. Experts fear that humans — instead of natural forces — may be causing some of these changes by burning fossil fuels and in this way pumping into the air huge quantities of gases, such as carbon dioxide.

Politicians and scientists everywhere are now studying the problem to see how we can stop, or at least limit, these changes. There are no easy answers because many scientists are still uncertain of the causes.

▲ Weather can change greatly from day to day. Top: Oak trees photographed at 1:30 PM on a gray day in April. Above: The same trees at 8:00 AM the following day. It had snowed during the night.

◀ Climates differ greatly. These two beaches were photographed during the same time of the year. Opposite: A beach in Norway that lies close to the Arctic Circle. Left: A beach in Sri Lanka in the tropics.

5

2: THE WEATHER MACHINE

What Makes the Weather?

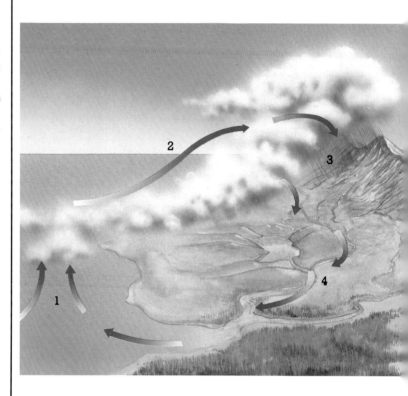

Most of the Earth's water is in the oceans and seas. It moves around the world in what is known as the water cycle. Sea-water evaporates into the air with the Sun's heat (1). It rises, cools, and condenses to form clouds (2). Some of these clouds produce rain (3). If the rain falls on land, in time the water finds its way back to the sea — in rivers, for example (4). ▶

Air pressure

The pressure at any place is the weight of the column of air above that place. The higher above sea level you are, the less air there is above you, and the lower the air pressure.

When air becomes warm, it gets lighter, or less dense. This means that changes in the temperature of the air affect the weather by changing the air pressure. But changes in air pressure are not linked directly to rising or falling temperatures because the atmosphere is so complicated.

You can think of the world's weather as being made by a machine, with the Sun as the fuel that powers it and the Earth's atmosphere as the machinery.

Just as heat from burning fuel drives a car's engine or a steam turbine, so the Sun heats the Earth's surface and "drives" its atmosphere. But it does this unevenly.

Because the Earth is shaped like a ball, the Sun's heat is greatest at the equator. There it has the least amount of air to travel through, and it covers the smallest surface area. At the poles, the Sun's heat comes toward Earth's surface at an angle, so it has to go through more air to reach the ground. The heat also spreads out over a larger area.

6

Land and sea

Land heats up more quickly than the sea, and it cools more quickly, too. In the tropics, land and sea are always very warm. In higher latitudes — toward the poles — the sea is cooler than the land in summer, but warmer than the land in winter.

These differences and the more direct heat from the Sun affect the temperature of the air, so there are always areas covered by warm air while other areas are covered by cold air. When heated air rises, cooler air from elsewhere blows in to take its place. This is the basic cause of the winds.

When the Sun heats the air, it also heats the sea, and some of the seawater evaporates — rises into the air as moisture. When this moist air rises higher, it cools off and the moisture condenses, or turns into droplets, to form clouds. If the clouds grow cooler, the water in them gathers into large drops or crystals that fall as rain, snow, or hail.

There are definite boundaries between masses of cold air and hot air, known as fronts. The rising air at these fronts results in clouds and rain.

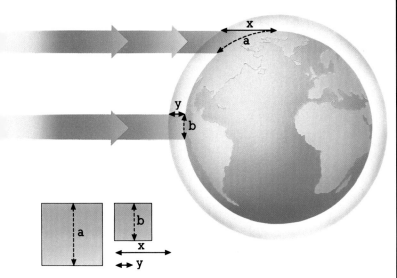

In an aneroid, or dry, barometer, variations in air pressure cause the disk to expand or contract, and this moves the spring and the attached pointer.

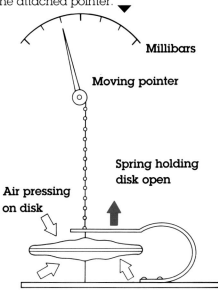

Millibars

Moving pointer

Spring holding disk open

Air pressing on disk

Disk containing partial vacuum

Did You Know?

Differences in air pressure are measured by an instrument called a barometer. In a mercury barometer, a column of mercury in a glass tube rises or falls with pressure changes. In an aneroid barometer, an airtight metal disk containing a partial vacuum expands or shrinks as pressure changes.

Pressure is measured either in millimeters of mercury in a barometer or in bars. The bar, usually divided into 1,000 millibars (mb), is a metric unit. One bar equals 750.1 mm (29.53 inches) of mercury.

◀ This diagram shows how heat from the Sun falls over a greater area of land at the poles (a) than at the equator (b). The heat also has to travel through more air (x) at the poles than at the equator (y).

7

Clouds

Fog and mist

Fog forms when water vapor condenses near the ground. It is composed of millions of tiny water droplets, much the same as in a cloud. If the droplets form around smoke, chemicals from car exhausts, or dirt, the result is smog, which often gathers over cities. Fog or smog can make it hard to see more than a short distance.

Mist is fog that is much less dense than usual, so you can see farther in it.

Mist often forms in valleys during clear, calm nights. Such a mist can last long after the Sun rises, as this picture taken in eastern France shows. ▼

How clouds form

When water is heated it turns into vapor, an invisible gas. If you boil water, it changes into gas, or steam, rapidly. But at ordinary temperatures, water becomes vapor slowly. This is called evaporation. The air often holds a great deal of water vapor from evaporation.

When heated air rises, it takes water vapor with it. Because the atmosphere usually grows cooler the higher you go, the vapor cools, too, and begins to condense, or turn back into water.

The air is full of tiny particles of dust and salt so small that you cannot see them. The water condenses in very tiny drops of liquid or ice crystals around these particles. This is how clouds are formed.

Kinds of clouds

There are ten different kinds of clouds. They have been given scientific names that describe them. The three basic types are cirrus, cumulus, and stratus.

The word *cirrus* means "a curl," and that is just what cirrus clouds look like — wispy curled threads in the sky. They are also known as mare's tails. These clouds float very high, sometimes higher than 32,800 feet (10,000 m) above the ground.

◀ Five of the most common types of clouds. From top to bottom, they are the high, streaky cirrus; the patchy gray-white altocumulus; the heavy cumulonimbus (the thunder-cloud); the cottony cumulus; and the gray, low-lying stratus — shown here hiding the top of the Eiffel Tower, 984 feet (300 m) tall, in Paris.

Ten cloud types

Cirrus: high, white featherlike clouds; often called mare's tails. They may indicate rain to come.

Cirrocumulus: thin cloud sheets forming ripples like sand ripples, or very small patches. Cold weather may follow.

Cirrostratus: nearly transparent, white cloud, often making halos around the Sun or the Moon. Rain or snow may be coming.

Altocumulus: gray-white cloud in sheets or patches. Changeable weather ahead.

Altostratus: gray, streaky cloud, often thin in places, that may cover the sky completely. It may warn of rain.

Nimbostratus: thick cloud, often dark, blotting out the Sun and usually producing rain or snow.

Stratocumulus: rolling masses of gray or white cloud with dark patches. Snow may come.

Stratus: usually gray, low-lying, uniform cloud, often producing drizzle; hides hilltops and even the tops of skyscrapers.

Cumulus: separate piles of cloud, rising into domes; may look like lumps of cotton. These are fair-weather clouds.

Cumulonimbus: heavy, towering storm cloud, very tall with a dark base; the thundercloud.

Cumulus means "a heap," and cumulus clouds appear as great heaps, towering up into the sky. With the Sun behind them, they appear dark, but when lighted from the front, they gleam white. They often form over land on fine days as warm air rises.

Stratus means "a layer," and stratus clouds form gray layers, usually closer to the ground.

Two more terms are used to describe clouds: *alto,* which means "high," and *nimbus,* which means "rain-bearing." But such clouds can bring snow as well. These five terms are combined to name the various kinds of clouds.

A rainbow forms when the Sun shines on raindrops in the sky. Each raindrop acts as a tiny prism, breaking the sunlight into the colors of the spectrum — red, orange, yellow, green, blue, and violet. ▼

Rain, Hail, and Snow

Precipitation sizes

The biggest raindrops are those that fall in a summer thunderstorm. They may be up to one-third of an inch (8 mm) across. Drizzle has the smallest drops — one-fiftieth of an inch (0.5 mm) or less across. The biggest snowflakes are up to 2 inches (50 mm) across. Those are the very wet ones that fall when the temperature is rising. Hailstones vary between one-fourth and one-half inch (6-13 mm). Some are over two inches (50 mm) across. The heaviest hailstones fell in Ohio in 1981, weighing up to 30 pounds (13.6 kg).

Meteorologists use the term *precipitation* for all the forms in which water falls from clouds. They have listed eleven different kinds of precipitation. But for most people there are just three — rain, hail, and snow.

They all start with tiny cloud droplets or ice particles joining together. One million droplets may form one raindrop. Some particles are water, and some are ice crystals, depending on the temperature at which they form.

How moisture falls

As the droplets grow bigger, they become heavy enough to fall to the ground. Particles of ice may melt and fall as rain if the air is warm enough, but if the air is cold, they fall as snow or hail. Snow is more common in cold winter weather. Hailstones, because they are heavy and fall rapidly, can reach the ground still frozen in spring or summer.

Rainfall is measured in millimeters with an instrument called a rain gauge. Rainfall is heaviest in the tropics. The great heat from the Sun there draws up large amounts of water to form clouds. Rainfall in the tropics often averages over 100 inches (2,500 mm) a year. In the temperate lands of the north, rainfall is much lower.

Rainfall can vary greatly even over a small landmass like Britain. In southeastern Britain, the rainfall may be less than 20 inches (500 mm) a year, while high mountains in the west can get ten times as much.

▲ Snowflakes form many different patterns, but their shape is always based on six sides.

Dew and frost

At night, when the Sun is no longer warming the ground, plants and other objects on the surface may become so cold that water vapor in the air condenses on them. If the vapor condenses as water, we get dew. If it condenses as ice, we have frost.

You can often see frost on the grass or on windows early on chilly mornings. This is because they became cold during the night and any vapor touching these cold surfaces turned to ice.

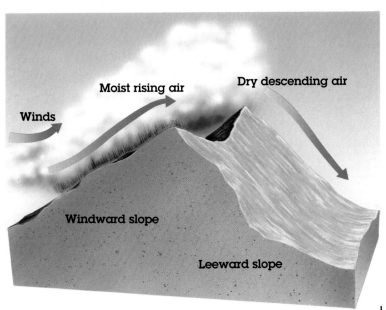

Moist rising air

Dry descending air

Winds

Windward slope

Leeward slope

◀ When moist air rises up against mountains, it forms clouds, and rain falls on the mountains' windward side. The air that crosses over and comes down on the other side is less moist, so the leeward side of the mountains is warmer and drier. This side is in a rain shadow.

Rain shadow

The northwestern coast of North America is wet because most of the rain-bearing winds come from the Pacific and shed their rain on the western slopes of the Rocky Mountains. The dry eastern side is said to be in a rain shadow. A similar rain shadow is cast westward by the Great Dividing Range of Australia's eastern coast. This rain shadow leaves much of that country's interior a desert.

Did You Know?

Rain sometimes falls from a cloudless sky. The reason for this is that the cloud disperses before the rain from it reaches the ground.

Wind, Highs, and Lows

This picture, taken from the US weather satellite *NOAA-9*, shows two depressions, or lows, over western Europe. These are the swirls of cloud over the North Sea and Sweden. The cloud spirals are caused by the way the winds blow around a low. Close to the low, these winds would be very strong and the weather bad. ▶

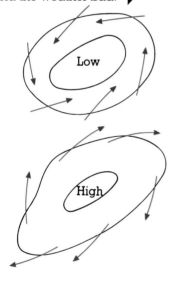

▲ This diagram shows how, in the Northern Hemisphere, winds spiral inward and counterclockwise around a center of low pressure. Around a high, winds spiral outward in a clockwise direction.

When warm air rises, the air pressure at ground level is lower. Wind blows inward toward centers of low pressure. But because the Earth is spinning around on its axis from west to east, the wind swerves. In the Northern Hemisphere, the winds blow off course to their right, and in the Southern Hemisphere, they blow in a curve to their left.

In the Northern Hemisphere, the wind blows around a center of low pressure in a direction

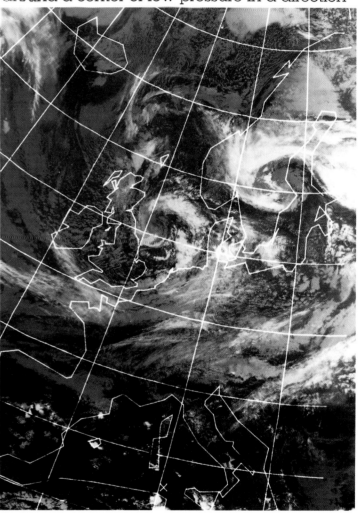

that is counterclockwise. But from a center of high pressure, the winds blow slightly outward and around in a clockwise direction. In the Southern Hemisphere, winds of highs and lows circle in directions opposite those in the north.

Fine weather or clouds

Centers of low pressure are called cyclones, or depressions, or just lows. High-pressure centers are called anticyclones, or highs. Lows nearly always have heavy clouds and strong winds. In a low, the weather may be dull, wet, and even stormy. Highs have just a few clouds and some light winds. So you can expect fine weather in a high.

Veering and backing

The wind does not blow evenly. Friction with the Earth's surface makes the wind gusty. Gusts are local winds. Places as close as 330 feet (100 m) apart may have different winds at the same time. When the wind is gusty, it generally changes direction. In the Northern Hemisphere, when the wind veers, it changes its direction clockwise. When the wind backs, it changes its direction counterclockwise.

On land in the Northern Hemisphere, winds tend to increase and veer during the day, and decrease and back during the night. Winds are steadier and less changeable over the open sea. In the Southern Hemisphere, wind changes direction in the opposite way.

Coastal breezes

In coastal areas, the wind is likely to change direction between day and night. The land heats quickly during the day, so the air above it gets warmer and rises. Air from over the sea is pulled inland, and a sea breeze sets in by late morning, dying away in the late evening as the land cools.

At night the sea remains warm while the land cools. Air rises from the sea, pulling cool land air seaward. This produces an offshore breeze. A land breeze helps a sailing ship to put out to sea, but a sea breeze makes it more difficult.

By day, the heat of the Sun warms the air over land, causing it to rise and bringing cooler air to blow onshore. High up, there is a weak flow of warm air in the opposite direction (dashed line). At night, the land becomes colder than the sea, and wind blows from the land to the sea. ▼

Storms

A tornado causes the greatest damage of all storms. It can carry large objects for a very long way. ▶

In a tropical storm, rising air in the cloud (1) draws in a rush of air farther down (2) while the "eye" (3) remains calm. At the upper levels, winds spiral outward (4). ▼

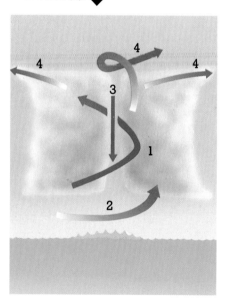

Did You Know?

The worst tropical storm ever recorded hit Bangladesh on October 12 and 13, 1970. It killed about a million people. The Tri-State Tornado, the deadliest in the United States, killed 689 people in Missouri, Illinois, and Indiana on March 18, 1925.

Winds grow strongest when a depression develops. Air sucked into the low at or near ground level is whirled around and upward and hurled out high above the ground. The deeper the depression, the more violent the winds become, and then a storm blows up. The word "storm" refers to severe winds with or without precipitation.

Tropical storms

Tropical storms bring violent weather. They develop over the sea, but may drift over land. They are common in three regions.

In the Caribbean Sea and the southern part of the North Atlantic, they are called hurricanes. In the Indian Ocean area, they are known as cyclones — Australians call them willy-willies. In the northern Pacific Ocean, we call them typhoons.

A tropical storm may be hundreds of miles across. The wind speed at its edge may be around 20 miles (32 km) per hour. Closer to

the center, the winds become more violent and may exceed 180 miles (290 km) per hour. In the hurricane's center — the "eye" of the storm — there is a complete calm.

A trail of destruction

Tropical storms do tremendous damage on land, destroying trees and crops and wrecking buildings. They drive huge waves onto coasts, causing damage and flooding.

Tornadoes have the most violent winds, but they average only one-half mile (800 m) across at ground level. A tornado is a column of wind whirling around at up to 500 miles (800 km) per hour. It usually has a dark thundercloud overhead.

As the whirling funnel rushes along, it sucks up everything in its path, even buildings, like a giant vacuum cleaner. A tornado can do more damage than a hurricane. The United States has about 1,000 tornadoes a year. A tornado over water is called a waterspout.

Thunderstorms

Thunderstorms develop in dark, towering cumulonimbus clouds. Violent currents of air rush up and down in these clouds, building up static electricity — just as you do if you brush your hair vigorously.

Eventually the electricity discharges in an enormous spark up to several miles within a cloud, between two or more clouds, between a cloud and the surrounding air, or between a cloud and the ground. This is lightning. Thunder is caused by the air suddenly heating, and expanding, from the lightning.

You can see lightning right away, but the thunder comes later because sound travels more slowly than light. You can tell how far away lightning is by counting the seconds between seeing the flash and hearing the thunder. Divide by five for the distance in miles, and by three for kilometers.

Lightning striking the CN Tower in Toronto. ▼

3: WEATHER FORECASTING

Reporting on the Weather

In order to forecast what the weather is going to be like, a meteorologist has to know what it's doing now, and where it's doing it. To find this out, he or she collects a series of observations from a wide area. These should all be made, as nearly as possible, at the same time.

The farther ahead the forecast is to be, the bigger the area from which observations must be collected. A forecast for any part of the world for three or four hours ahead needs weather information that comes from over 300 miles (500 km) around.

To forecast the weather three or four days ahead, the forecaster needs to have data from the whole hemisphere.

Country lore

There are many old country sayings about the weather, but most have little foundation in fact, such as this one:

Red sky at night,
Sailor's delight;
Red sky in the morning,
Sailors take warning.

While a soft, red night sky can mean good weather tomorrow, and a cloudy, red morning sky may bring rain, neither is always true.

In North America, people say that if the groundhog can see its own shadow on February 2, there will be six more weeks of winter.

A North American groundhog, or woodchuck. Tradition says that whether or not the groundhog sees its shadow indicates when winter will end. ▶

Taking a global view

Weather systems are moving around and affecting each other all over the globe. A northern meteorologist who wants to forecast the weather more than five days ahead needs information from the Southern Hemisphere. It is almost impossible to forecast more than ten days ahead because too many unforeseen changes can take place.

To predict the weather, a forecaster needs information on the wind, temperature, air pressure, humidity, clouds, precipitation, and visibility. The observations are easy to make. Anyone can operate a simple weather station.

The reports come from a variety of sources. Human observers provide the main facts, and they are supplemented by reports from automatic weather stations, ships at sea, airliners in flight, automatic weather buoys, radar stations, equipment carried aloft by balloons, and photographs taken by satellites.

▲ A Stevenson screen. This standard housing, about four feet (1.2 m) above the ground, provides shade and ventilation for the instruments that measure and continuously record humidity, and maximum and minimum temperatures.

This weather ship monitors changes in temperature, wind, humidity, and air pressure. ▼

Radar, Balloons, and Satellites

Radar scanners constantly sweep the skies, picking up information about clouds and rain. They can detect the difference between heavy and light rain.

Weather balloons filled with hydrogen or helium carry instruments called radiosondes. These sample conditions high above the ground and give a three-dimensional picture of the weather. The radiosondes broadcast information to surface receivers. Radar tracks the position of each balloon. When a balloon rises to nearly 20 miles (30 km), it will usually burst. This is because the air pressure outside it is less than the pressure inside. The radio-sonde parachutes back to the ground.

Space watch

On April 1, 1960, the United States launched *Tiros I*, the first weather satellite. Since then, a satellite network has been built up to keep a

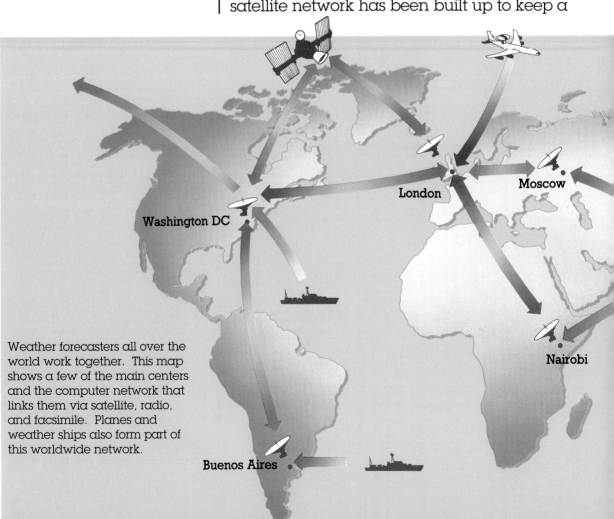

Weather forecasters all over the world work together. This map shows a few of the main centers and the computer network that links them via satellite, radio, and facsimile. Planes and weather ships also form part of this worldwide network.

London

Moscow

Washington DC

Nairobi

Buenos Aires

continuous watch on the world's weather. These weather satellites take pictures as they orbit Earth. They beam these pictures to a command station on the ground. There, a computer adds the outlines of coasts to the pictures. You can see these outlines as white lines on televised weather satellite pictures.

The command station beams these pictures back to the satellite, which relays them to all the receiving stations over the area it covers.

Keeping in touch

Ordinary communications satellites transmit weather pictures and data that go far beyond the local command stations. Weather information isn't helpful unless it can be gathered quickly for immediate use. Local information must arrive within about half an hour. Data from the other side of the world must come in to the forecaster within three to six hours.

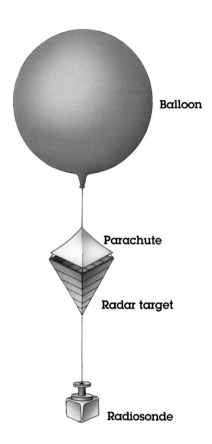

Balloon

Parachute

Radar target

Radiosonde

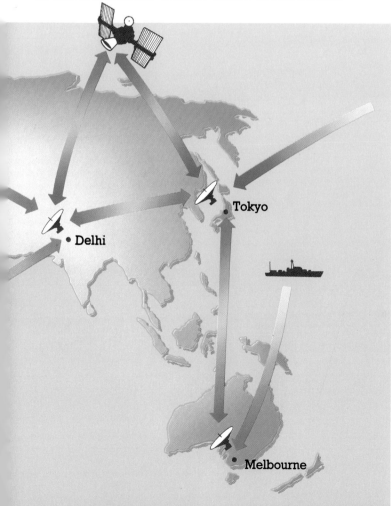

▲ A weather balloon carries a radiosonde, an instrument that monitors weather conditions high above the ground and radios the information back to Earth. Its radar target enables it to be tracked from the ground. When the balloon finally bursts, the parachute gently carries the equipment down to the surface. If the radiosonde is recovered, it can be used again.

Computer network

The fastest communication is through computer networks that can send and receive huge amounts of information.

Computers connect all the major meteorological centers throughout the world.

Putting It All Together

Human beings can work out a reasonable forecast over a limited area for up to 18 hours ahead. But for larger areas and for longer periods, the task is so complicated that they must use computers to do a lot of the work.

Mathematical calculations

The key to most forecasts is observing highs and lows. The way they move indicates changes of wind direction that, in turn, may produce changes of temperature. The computer makes calculations and prints out a chart of the probable pressure patterns. The chart is marked in an international code so that other countries can use it, too.

Pressure points

Next, those swirling lines are added to the map. These lines are called isobars, from the

This flow chart shows how all the information about the weather is gathered together to bring you the daily forecast. ▶

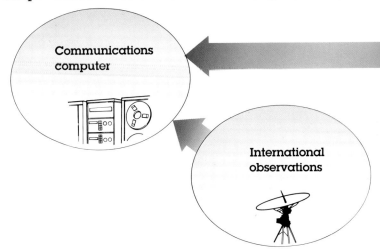

Communications computer

International observations

Points of equal pressure are plotted on a map and then joined by lines called isobars. The numbers given are in millibars. ▼

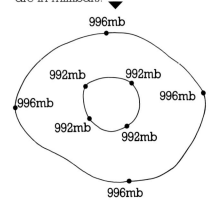

996mb
992mb   992mb
996mb   996mb
992mb   992mb
996mb

Greek word *isos*, meaning "equal." Isobars join points where the pressure, measured in millibars, is equal. These lines are similar to the contour lines on a geographic map that join points of equal height.

The forecaster studies the chart, comparing it with a series of satellite pictures showing the recent movement of clouds. Then he or she has to decide what is likely to happen next.

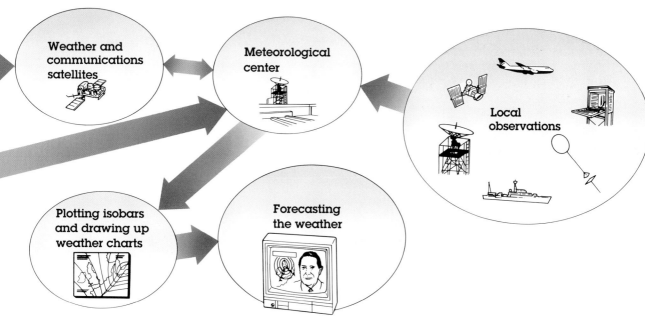

These decisions are not easy to make. The weather seems to change course as unpredictably as a group of children running around a school playground! But forecasts are right most of the time. When they seem to be wrong, it's often a matter of timing. It's hard to predict the speed at which a weather system is moving, so rain often doesn't arrive when it is expected, but turns up hours earlier or later.

▲ Top: A weather forecaster at work, surrounded by banks of computers and visual display terminals that show all the information that is coming in from around the world.

Reading a Weather Map

This chart shows a typical weather pattern for northwestern Europe. The key helps us read the plotted isobars and observations. In the west, there are clouds, rain, and showers, along with high winds around the area of low pressure and its associated fronts. But in the east, high pressure leads to clear skies — except where light winds allow mist to form. Wind speeds are measured in knots — nautical miles per hour. ▶

At first sight, a weather chart may look confusing, but the signs and symbols on it are really very exact. With practice, a person can easily read even the charts that meteorologists use themselves. These contain much more detail than the charts you see in newspapers or on television weather reports.

Look for the highs and lows. Even if they are not labeled, you can pick them out by seeing how close the isobars are. If they are close together, you are probably looking at a low, where pressure changes rapidly. You can expect high winds and rain with a low.

Highs have widely spaced isobars, and generally signify clear weather. In winter they may indicate frost or fog.

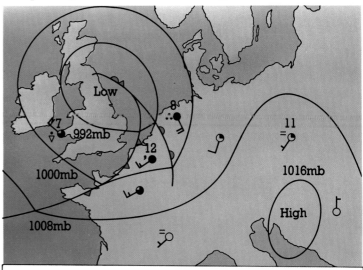

Fronts	Cloud Amount	Weather
▷ Warm front	● Full cover (overcast)	∴ Rain
▶ Cold front	◑ 3/4 cover	' Drizzle
▶ Occluded front	◔ 1/4 cover	▽ Showers
		= Mist
Winds		
┴ 5 knots	Figures above the "cloud" symbols are temperatures in degrees Celsius	Isobars are labeled in millibars
┗ 10 knots		
┗╴ 15 knots		
┗╸ 20 knots		

Useful forecasts

Everybody is interested in the weather, but some people need particular information.

For example, farmers need to know when conditions favor the spread of pests and diseases, and those with livestock need advance warning of snow so they can get their animals to shelter or take feed to them.

Offshore oil rigs, risky in high winds and waves, get special forecasts. Gas and electricity suppliers need to know when the weather will be cold so they can provide more power.

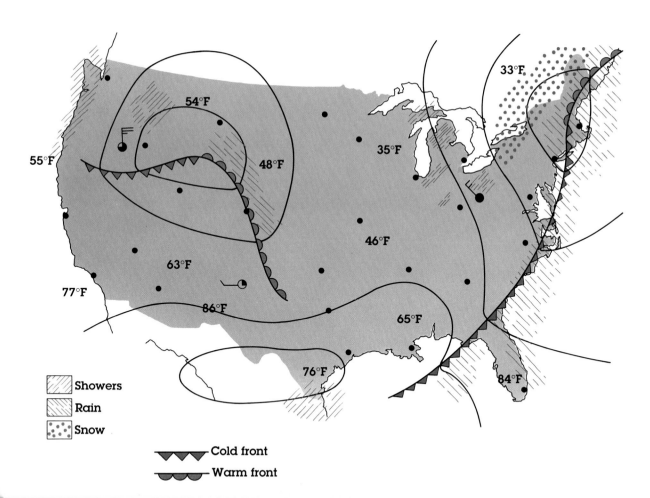

Showers

Rain

Snow

Cold front

Warm front

54°F
55°F
48°F
35°F
33°F
46°F
63°F
77°F
86°F
65°F
76°F
84°F

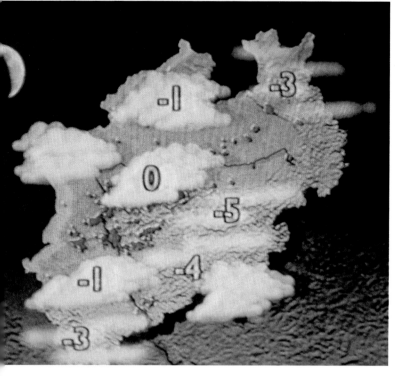

▲ A newspaper weather map for an April day in the United States. The East Coast has rain associated with a cold front. There is rain turning to snow in the northeast, associated with low pressure, a warm front, and temperatures close to freezing. Over the Southwest lies an area of high pressure, with temperatures as high as 86°F (30°C). In the Northwest, the weather becomes cooler, with rain along a warm front and showers farther north.

◀ TV weather maps, like this one for a region in Germany, are even simpler. A forecaster explains them.

4: | CLIMATE

The World's Climates

Many of the important differences in the world are due to varying climates. Climate affects the kinds of plants and animals that can thrive in an area. Climate also helps to shape the local landscape.

Climate affects people. It influences the way they live, dress, and work. It even changes their bodies because over thousands of years people have altered genetically to suit the part of the world they live in.

Many climatologists agree on twelve different climates. Today's scientific methods use other ways of classifying climates. These new classifications rely on statistics and also on

Main climate types

Icecap: always below freezing; sometimes snows.

Polar: cold, with a short, chilly summer; little precipitation.

Subarctic: long, cold winters and short, cool summers; light to moderate precipitation.

Steppe: great changes from hot to cold except near coasts; little precipitation.

Highland: always cooler than surrounding climate zones.

Continental moist: cold winters, warm or cool summers; moderate precipitation.

Oceanic moist: cool winters, warm summers; moderate precipitation.

Desert: great changes from hot by day to cold at night; little precipitation.

Subtropical dry summer: mild, wet winters, and summers that are hot and dry.

Subtropical moist: cool winters, warm to hot summers; moderate precipitation.

Tropical wet and dry: hot, with a dry season and a very wet season.

Tropical wet: hot and wet all year round.

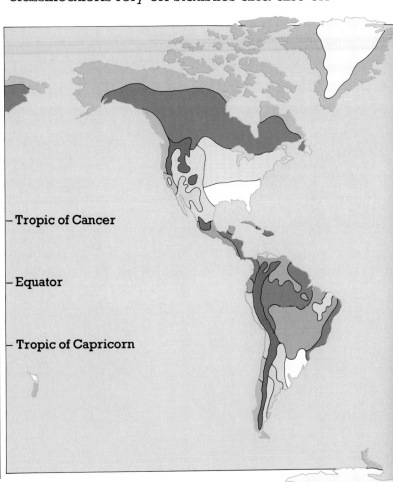

— Tropic of Cancer

— Equator

— Tropic of Capricorn

information gathered by satellites. But the original twelve are a convenient classification for everyday use. You will find them in the panel on the opposite page.

Climates range from cold and dry at the polar ice caps through hot and dry in the deserts to hot and wet near the equator. Within each climate zone there are many variations. For example, the north central and northeastern states are in a continental moist climate zone, but Minnesota has long, cold, snowy winters, while Maryland has shorter and milder winters with little snow.

Kenya lies in the tropics on the equator. The coastal region around Mombasa is hot and humid, but the highlands around Nairobi are a good 16°F (9°C) cooler, and the highest mountain in the country, Mount Kenya, has glaciers on its upper slopes.

▲ Mount Kenya lies almost on the equator. Its snowy peaks and glaciated slopes contrast with the warm grasslands below. This difference shows how there can be great variations in climate in one area.

Protective coloring

People who live in places with hot climates, such as the Pacific islands, the Mediterranean area, and Africa, tend to have dark skin. They have developed genetically so their skin contains extra melanin, a dark pigment that helps to protect them from the harmful ultraviolet rays of the Sun.

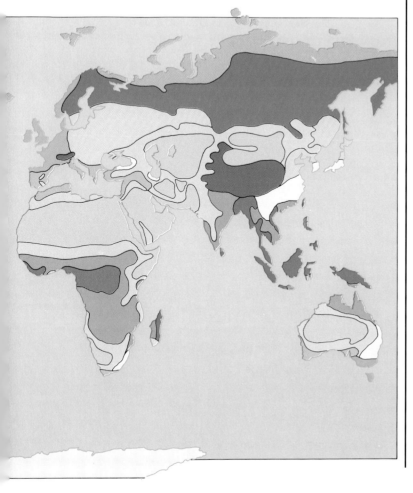

◀ This map shows the world's climatic regions colored according to the climate chart on the opposite page. Although the equatorial region receives the most heat from the Sun, you will see that the main areas of desert lie well to the north and south of the equator. The oceanic moist climate of western Europe is matched in only a few other areas of the world.

Sea and Land

The sea covers nearly three-quarters of the Earth's surface. It stays at a steadier temperature than the land and has a great effect on climate. Coastal areas have less variation in temperature than inland areas. Ocean currents can strengthen this effect.

Most surface currents are caused partly by the rotation of the Earth and partly by the wind that drives the surface water along. Tides also produce some currents.

Currents flow both deep in the ocean and on the surface. Deep currents flow from cold polar regions toward the warmer equator.

The Gulf Stream

Ocean currents affect the weather and climate of coastal regions. The Gulf Stream takes warm water from the Gulf of Mexico northward to become the North Atlantic Drift. This current crosses the North Atlantic and warms the shores of the British Isles, France, Norway, and Iceland.

This map shows the major warm and cold sea currents of the world. Their basic cause is the movement of deep, cold water from the poles toward the equator, and the movement of warm water near the surface away from the equatorial region. ▼

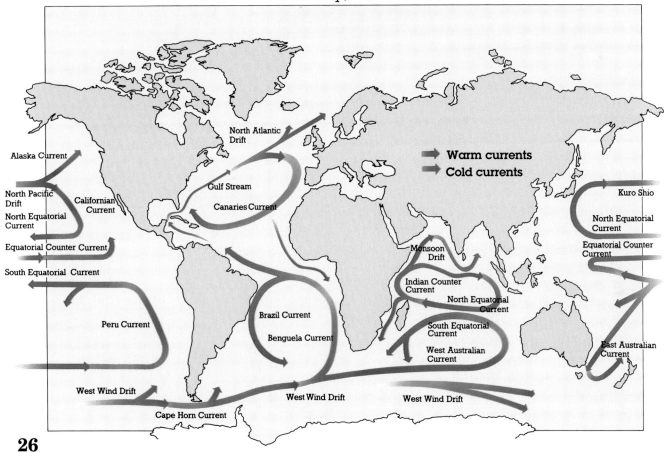

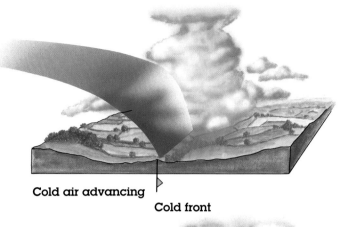

Cold air advancing

Cold front

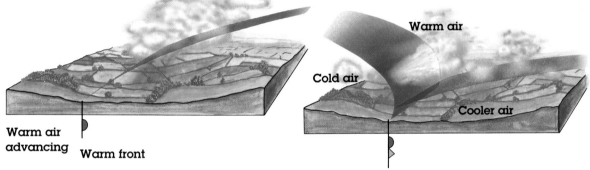

Warm air advancing

Warm front

Warm air

Cold air

Cooler air

Occluded front

▲ The weather patterns associated with cold, warm, and occluded fronts. Below each diagram is the symbol used to represent that front on a weather map. A cold front brings clouds and rain, but when it has passed, the rain usually stops. As a warm front advances, the clouds get lower, and rain or snow may fall. An occluded front may bring rain, but it is hard to predict the outcome of this complex weather pattern.

The huge northern landmasses of Eurasia and North America heat up in summer and get very cold in winter. For many months of the year, snow and ice cover vast areas of Siberia, Canada, and parts of the United States.

Air masses

A southerly wind in Europe will usually be warm because its air has crossed the hot Sahara Desert. Large volumes of air, known as air masses, move around the world. They can be hot or cold according to where they are, or have just been. An air mass that has been near the equator is warm; one that comes from one of the poles is cold.

The boundary between two air masses is called a front. Some fronts are very definite, but in other fronts the temperature of one air mass blends into another. Fronts are always moving. If warm air pushes out cold air, we experience a warm front. If a cold front pushes out warm air, we have a cold front. And if the cold front pushes the warm air mass above the cold air so that the cold front faces another cold air mass, the front is occluded.

El Niño

El Niño is a warm Pacific current flowing east every two to seven years around Christmas. It blocks the flow of rising, plankton-rich cold water from the Antarctic up the west coast of South America. This affects the world's weather system, causing droughts, storms, and floods in places that normally do not have them.

The World's Winds

The world's major wind zones.
The horse latitudes and the
doldrums are regions of calms,
with little or no wind. But
sudden storms can blow up. ▶

▲ An anemometer on the top of a
tower at Jodrell Bank Observatory
in northern England. The radio
telescope in the background is
among the world's largest.

Many local winds may blow for a day or two
at a time, but in the world's major wind zones,
the winds blow steadily in one direction most
of the time. These steady winds are known as
prevailing winds.

For about 680 miles (1,100 km) on either
side of the equator, where the temperature is
generally highest, there are no prevailing
winds. This is a region of calms and light,
changing winds called the doldrums.

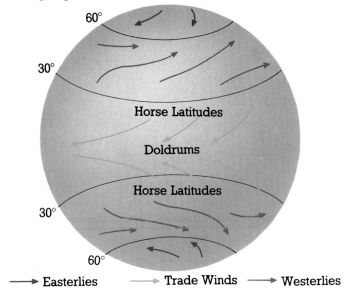

The trade winds

There are two regions of trade winds, one
north and one south of the doldrums. These
winds blow toward the equator and slightly
from the east. Their name comes from the
days of trading ships that relied on them for
power as traders sailed around the world.

At about 30° latitude on either side of the
equator lie two other belts of calms. These are
called the horse latitudes, possibly because
any horses aboard becalmed sailing ships
died of thirst when water supplies ran low.

North and south of the horse latitudes lie the
prevailing westerlies. In the Northern Hemisphere, these winds bring weather from across
the Pacific Ocean to North America. The
westerlies usually blow slightly away from the
equator, but they are quite variable from day

to day. Finally, near the poles lie the prevailing easterlies. These winds blow slightly outward from the poles.

Measuring the wind

The most common instrument for measuring wind speed is the anemometer. It has three, four, or six cups on spokes that spin in the wind. The speed the cups revolve at is the wind speed, which is read from a meter.

The Beaufort Wind Force Scale

Wind speed is indicated by force numbers from 0 to 12. The scale given here is the one used on land. British admiral Sir Francis Beaufort invented the wind force scale in 1805.

No.	Name	Speed in mph (kph)	Effects of wind
0	Calm	**Under 1 (<1)**	Smoke rises straight
1	Light air	**1-3 (1-5)**	Smoke shows wind direction
2	Light breeze	**4-7 (6-11)**	Wind felt on face
3	Gentle breeze	**8-12 (12-19)**	Paper and dry leaves move; flags fly out
4	Moderate breeze	**13-18 (20-28)**	Dust and small branches move
5	Fresh breeze	**19-24 (29-38)**	Flags flap, small leafy trees sway
6	Strong breeze	**25-31 (39-49)**	Large branches sway
7	Moderate gale	**32-38 (50-61)**	Whole trees sway
8	Gale	**39-46 (62-74)**	Difficult walking into wind; twigs break
9	Strong gale	**47-54 (75-88)**	Branches on ground; shingles blow off
10	Storm	**55-63 (89-102)**	Trees fall; buildings heavily damaged
11	Violent storm	**64-73 (103-117)**	Widespread damage
12	Hurricane	**Over 73 (>117)**	Buildings destroyed

◀ Strong prevailing winds can shape the growth of trees, as shown here, where the wind generally blows from the right of the picture.

Winds blow

Wind directions are always named after the direction the wind comes from. So the westerlies blow from the west, and the easterlies blow from the east. Ocean currents are named differently.

▲ Clouds in a jet stream over Egypt and the Red Sea were photographed from the US spacecraft *Gemini 12*.

Jet streams

Jet streams are high-altitude air currents, usually at 30,000 to 50,000 feet (9,000-15,000 m). They travel at speeds up to over 250 miles (400 km) per hour. These streams affect the speed of any aircraft flying in or near them. There are five main jet streams. One just north of the equator travels, in summer only, from east to west. The other four jets flow from west to east, two in each hemisphere. Strong jet streams occur near fronts and depressions. When high, fast-moving clouds can be seen, changeable weather is often on its way.

What Brings the Seasons?

The changing seasons have a dramatic effect on plant life in temperate regions. Below: The fresh green colors of trees early in a New England summer. ▼

Opposite: In fall, the same trees change to rich reds and golds just before the leaves drop off for the winter. ▶ ▶

To understand the seasons, you have to know something about how the Earth moves. It rotates around the Sun, taking a year to complete the journey.

At the same time, the Earth is spinning around once a day on its own axis, like a bicycle wheel on its axle. But the Earth's spin is not parallel to the path it takes around the Sun. It is tilted at about 23.5°.

The Sun heats the Earth hotter at the equator than at the poles. The diagram on the opposite page shows how different parts of the Earth receive more sunlight at certain times of the year than at others.

Summer and winter

When the North Pole is tilted toward the Sun, the Northern Hemisphere has summer, and the Southern Hemisphere has winter. When the North Pole is tilted away from the Sun, the Southern Hemisphere has summer and it is winter in the Northern Hemisphere.

The tropics lie in the region between the Tropic of Cancer and the Tropic of Capricorn. This area has much the same amount of sunlight all year round. The tropics do not have summer and winter. Instead, they have a wet season and a dry season.

If you look at a map, you will see that most

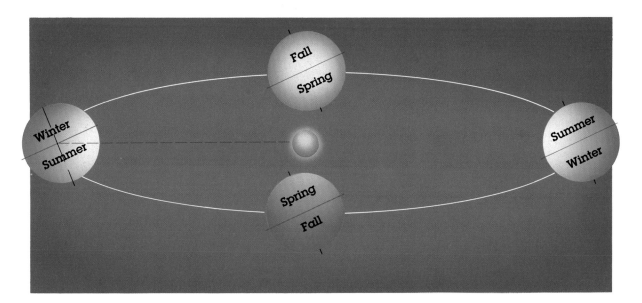

of the world's land lies in the Northern Hemisphere. Because land gains and loses heat rapidly, the northern half of the world has more variations and extremes of temperature and weather than the southern half has.

Day and night

As the Earth rotates, it turns toward the Sun and away from it, causing day and night. At the equator, day and night are almost equal in length. Farther north and south, days are much shorter in winter and longer in summer because of the Earth's tilt. Longer nights help to make the weather colder.

▲ Places on the Earth receive differing amounts of sunlight during the year because the Earth's axis is tilted at an angle to its path around the Sun. This produces the seasons. When it is summer in the Northern Hemisphere, it is winter in the Southern Hemisphere. Six months later, this is reversed. There are more hours of daylight in summer than in winter.

What Makes a Climate?

Slopes facing north and south have different climates, as shown by these two views of a pass in the Pyrenees, photographed on the same day in late summer. Below, left: The slope on the northern, French, side is still covered with snow, even in the summertime. Below, right: On the southern, Spanish, side, there is no snow. ▼

There are many reasons why climates vary from place to place. Like the weather, climates are the result of the Earth's surface being heated by the Sun and cooling down at night. The movement of the world's ocean currents also affects climate because their warm or cold waters heat or cool the air.

A tiny amount of heat comes from inside the Earth, but not enough to affect climate. But the Earth gives off heat that it gains from the Sun. The gains and losses are different from place to place. The resulting effect is called the radiation balance. This is the over-all loss or gain of heat in a place.

Gains and losses of heat

The latitude of a place — where it is north or south of the equator — affects these gains and losses. As we found earlier, the surface of the Earth receives the most sunlight near the equator. The amount the surface gets gradually decreases as you go toward the poles.

The atmosphere acts as a buffer for both

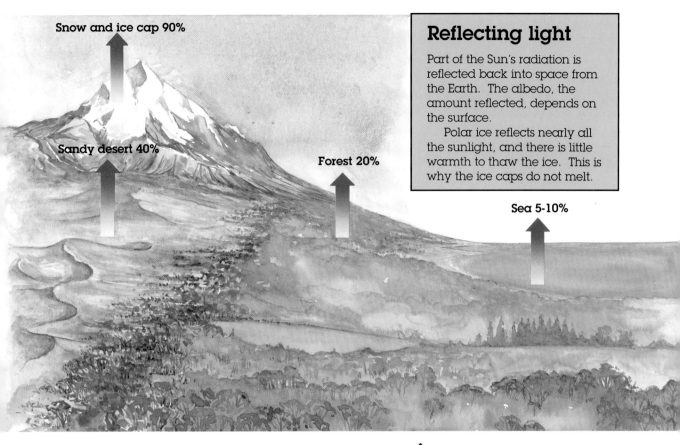

Snow and ice cap 90%

Sandy desert 40%

Forest 20%

Sea 5-10%

Reflecting light

Part of the Sun's radiation is reflected back into space from the Earth. The albedo, the amount reflected, depends on the surface.

Polar ice reflects nearly all the sunlight, and there is little warmth to thaw the ice. This is why the ice caps do not melt.

incoming and outgoing heat. Locally, cloud cover makes a big difference, and so does the amount of soot and other pollutants in the air. The Sun never shines as brightly through an industrial haze as it does where the air is clear.

The sea forms a huge reservoir of stored heat. This is why coastal areas tend to have more moderate climates than places in the middle of continents. Even huge lakes will have an effect on the local weather. The direction the wind blows and where it is coming from affect the temperature and rainfall.

Slopes facing north and south

A lot depends on which way the land slopes. Land that faces south in the Northern Hemisphere, and north in the Southern Hemisphere, receives more sunlight than the opposite slopes. The extra warmth and light means that plant life has a greater chance of flourishing on these slopes. Many farmers use this knowledge when planting their crops.

▲ This shows the percentage of the Sun's light that is reflected by different surfaces.

An experimental solar power station in Sicily. The Sun's heat is so intense that it can be used to generate electricity. ▼

The Unquiet Sun

This exaggerated diagram shows the Earth's elliptical orbit and its nearest and farthest positions from the Sun. ▼

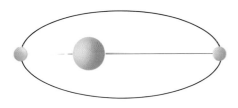

- - - - Distance at perihelion
_____ Distance at aphelion

This picture illustrates the constantly changing surface of the Sun. It shows a solar prominence, a loop of gas that may reach 20,000 miles (32,000 km) above the Sun's surface. This one erupted for over two hours. It was photographed in December 1973 from the US space station *Skylab*. The gas was glowing at a temperature of 36,000°F (20,000°C), with some strands reaching about 126,000°F (70,000°C). Water boils at only 212°F (100°C). ▶

The Sun produces a steady amount of heat. But the heat reaching the Earth varies. One reason is that the Earth's position in relation to the Sun is always changing.

The Earth's orbit is not a circle, but an ellipse — a flattened circle. The Sun is not at the center of the ellipse, but a little closer to one end of it. So during the year, the Earth moves closer to and farther from the Sun. When the Earth is closest to the Sun, we say it is at perihelion. When it is farthest away, it is at aphelion. The difference between perihelion and aphelion is about 2.5 million miles (4 million km). The Earth's tilt in relation to its path around the Sun changes over thousands of years, bringing a change in climate.

Sunspot activity
The Sun sends out a continuous stream of electrically charged cosmic particles, called the solar wind. The force of the solar wind grows stronger or weaker at times.

The solar wind is strongest during sunspot activity, especially when a solar flare occurs toward the end of a period of sunspot activity.

Sunspots reach their greatest number about every 11 years. Every 22 years, this peak number is much higher. These periods vary at times and may be as little as nine years or as much as 14 years apart.

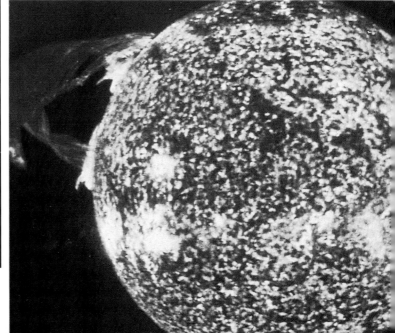

The aurora borealis, or northern lights, photographed near Fairbanks, Alaska. These strange lights happen when electrically charged subatomic particles — smaller than an atom — from the Sun act on atoms and molecules in the Earth's upper atmosphere. They occur at 62 to 190 miles (100-300 km) above the ground. Auroras are concentrated over the poles by the Earth's magnetic field.

Sunspot facts

Sunspots are dark patches that appear from time to time on the Sun's surface. The Sun is a huge ball of burning gases, a vast nuclear furnace. It has a magnetic field, like a gigantic bar magnet, and changes in this magnetic field result in sunspots.

When sunspot activity is greatest, we see auroras. The flickering lights in the far northern sky are called the aurora borealis, or northern lights. In the far south, they are the aurora australis. Sunspots upset magnetic compasses and interfere with radio and TV.

Warning: Never look at the Sun without special protection. The Sun can blind you. Neither sunglasses nor smoked glass will protect your eyes.

Why there is less rain

There seems to be reduced rainfall just after periods of great sunspot activity. There are some indications that sunspot "super peaks" occur about every 90 and 200 years. These may produce changes in climate.

Tides on Earth are caused by the pull of the Moon, and very high tides result from the combined pull of the Moon and the Sun. The planets cause tides in the gases that make up the Sun. Since what happens on the Sun affects our climate, climatologists must study events in space to find out what is happening, or may happen, on Earth.

Volcanoes and Meteorites

Scientists believe that this large crater at Gosse Bluff, Australia, was made by a meteorite that collided with the Earth millions of years ago. ▼

Near misses

Earth has had at least two near misses with asteroids in recent years. Hermes, only one mile (1.6 km) across, missed Earth by just 500,000 miles (800,000 km) in 1937. This is about twice the distance from the Earth to the Moon, considered very close in the vastness of space. In 1989, another asteroid came within a million miles (1.6 million km) of Earth.

An erupting volcano sends streams of red-hot lava pouring down its sides. Lava is the erupted form of magma, the molten rock that exists many miles down inside the Earth. A volcano also hurls forth a cloud of ash, gas, steam, dust, and lumps of rock. ▶

An erupting volcano can produce a dense haze. Mount St. Helens, in Washington State, blew up in 1980 and shot about one-half cubic mile (2 cu km) of dust into the air. Volcanic dust is so fine that you could line up over 50,000 dust particles side by side along one inch (2.5 cm) on your ruler. Imagine how many particles Mount St. Helens blew out!

The Mount St. Helens eruption wasn't the largest known. Cosigüina, in Nicaragua, in 1835 shot out 4.8 cubic miles (20 cu km) of dust. And Tamboru, in Indonesia, threw up 36.4 cubic miles (151.6 cu km) of dust in 1815. Volcanoes also spew forth huge quantities of sulfur dioxide and carbon dioxide gases.

Scientists think that the combined result of volcanic eruptions over the years has a cooling effect on climate, at least temporarily.

Missiles from space

Very large meteorites from outer space can produce even bigger dust clouds. A number of prehistoric meteorite craters have been identified, such as Barringer Meteor Crater in northern Arizona, which is 4,150 feet (1,265 m) in diameter. Much larger is a depression that is 275 miles (442 km) wide, found on the shore of Hudson Bay in the 1950s.

The Hudson Bay crater may have resulted from a collision with an asteroid, one of the numerous small bodies that orbit the Sun in a belt between Mars and Jupiter.

A collision of that size could send up a cloud of debris that would screen out sunlight for several years, killing plants and animals. Such a collision may have caused the extinction of the dinosaurs.

◀ One of the many dramatic sunsets painted by English artist Joseph Turner (1775-1851). This scene was probably painted at Rouen, France.

Turner's sunsets

The dust veil from a large eruption may persist for years, producing spectacular sunsets. The dramatic sunsets painted by the nineteenth-century English artist Joseph Turner may have been caused by volcanic dust, possibly from Tamboru and, later, Cosigüina.

Climate and Plants

Coniferous forest

Mediterranean scrub

Temperate broad-leaved forest

Equatorial and tropical rain forest

Grassland

Semidesert

Desert

Tundra and alpine

Ice desert

▲ Tundra and alpine vegetation near a lake in Alaska.

▲ Coniferous forest, found mostly in cooler lands.

Equatorial and tropical rain forest, found in hot lands. ▼

◀ Temperate broad-leaved forest with trees like oak and beech.

Climate determines what plants can thrive in an area, and also what animals can live there. For example, in the tundra of the far north, summers are short and winters are long, with snow covering the marshy land. No trees grow in the tundra, which lies north of the tree line — roughly the line of the Arctic Circle.

The only plants that can survive in the tundra are small, low-growing species. Mosses and lichens flourish, and other plants have a very short flowering season. Migrating animals move to the tundra in summer to graze on these plants.

Antarctica, the frozen southern continent, lies almost completely inside the Antarctic Circle. Mosses, lichens, and just three kinds of flowering plants grow in a few places near the coast. About 50 species of very tiny insects, spiders, and other creatures survive there.

In the temperate regions of the world, which

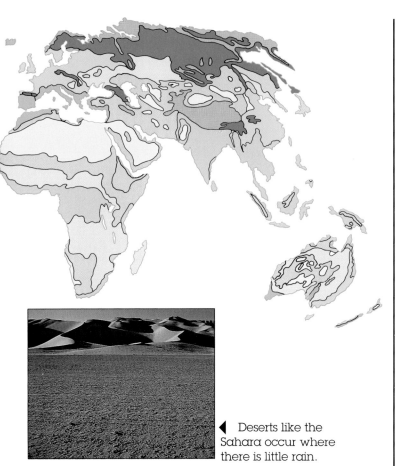

▲ Ice desert in Greenland, where little or nothing grows.

▲ Grassland flourishes where few trees can grow.

◀ Deserts like the Sahara occur where there is little rain.

lie between the Arctic and Antarctic circles and the tropics, grow forests of broad-leaved trees in the warmer areas. Large, grassy prairies are also widespread.

In the tropics, where the climate is warm and wet, forest trees grow to great heights. This region has the largest number of different plants and animals in the world.

The higher, the colder

Altitude can have the same effect as moving to the north or south, because the higher you go, the colder it becomes. The Himalaya Mountains are snow-covered all year round, even though they lie at the same latitude as North Africa and Florida and receive the same amount of daylight.

A mountain's tree line marks the limit of tree growth. The climate where the mountain is located determines the height of its tree line.

▲ Semideserts have a few hardy plants, such as giant cacti.

▲ Mediterranean scrub — woody shrubs also called maquis.

Climate and Animals

Like plants, animals have adapted to the climates of the places where they live. In regions with long, cold winters, animals such as musk oxen and polar bears have heavy fur, and their winter coats are generally thicker than their summer coats.

Some animals, such as the Arctic fox, grow a white winter coat that hides them in the snow-covered landscape.

Many animals hibernate in winter, passing the time in a deep sleep. Before hibernation, they eat heartily and store up extra fat to last them through the cold months, when they cannot find food.

Seasonal travelers

Many animals migrate to avoid harsh winters. The best-known migrants are birds. Many birds fly north in spring, when there are plenty of insects to provide them with food. They fly south again to tropical lands after they have reared their chicks.

Other birds fly south to Australia and New Zealand in spring, and return to the tropics in the autumn. The longest journeys of all are

This North African jerboa, or desert rat, stays underground by day to protect itself from the desert Sun. In cooler climates, animals may live in burrows in order to keep warm. Burrows also protect many animals from their predators. ▼

A camel is adapted to desert life. It stores food, in the form of fat, in the hump on its back, and it can go for days without drinking. Its large feet will not sink into the sand. Long, curly eyelashes protect its eyes.

The ermine, also called the weasel, is one of many animals that grows a white coat in winter. In its summer coat, it would show against the snow.

This dormouse, of northern Europe, hibernates in winter.

made by the Arctic tern. It spends the northern summer in the Arctic, and then flies south to the Antarctic Peninsula to enjoy the southern summer. This means it makes a record round trip totaling 25,000 miles (40,000 km)!

Desert animals have to cope with heat instead of cold. Many animals, such as the jerboas of the Sahara and the kangaroo rats of the North American deserts, escape the Sun's heat by burrowing into the sand, coming out at night to hunt for food.

White storks gather, ready to migrate. Many birds spend the winter months in warm lands, then fly to cooler places to nest and have their young.

41

5: CHANGES IN CLIMATE

Studying Climate Changes

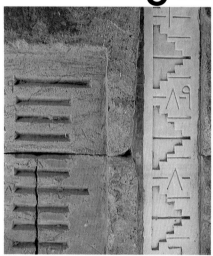

▲ A nilometer, on the Nile River at Aswan, measured water levels.

Old instruments

Instruments that measure weather conditions have been in existence for less than 400 years. The thermometer was invented in 1592, the barometer in 1643, and the rain gauge and the wind gauge in the 1600s.

One indicator of climate is the flow of rivers. The ancient Egyptians used nilometers to measure how high the Nile rose during the yearly flood. These were gauges that were carved in stone at intervals along the banks of the Nile River. Some of them have survived.

We can see climate changes going on today. An outstanding example is the behavior of the monsoon winds. These winds bring rains each year on which the countries of southern Asia and Africa depend.

If the monsoons fail to bring rain, crops do not grow, and people starve. But world wind patterns are changing. Since the 1960s, the seasonal rains have repeatedly failed over large parts of Africa, causing famines.

Changes in the past

If we understand what has happened in the past, we may be able to learn what is likely to happen in the future. The scientific study of weather and climate began only 300 years ago. But fortunately there are plenty of

references to the weather in old books, diaries, letters, and other documents.

Using these, climatologists have been able to piece together a jigsawlike picture of weather in Europe for at least a thousand years, and in China for five thousand years.

Trees help greatly in studying past climates. A tree adds a ring to its trunk for every year it lives — a thin ring in dry years, a thick ring in wet years. By comparing ring patterns in old, recently felled trees with those in timber from buildings, scientists have built up records that go back several thousand years.

Buried clues

Other clues to the past lie buried in the ground for archaeologists and geologists to find. The mud at the bottom of lakes often preserves plant debris, such as pollen, that shows whether warm-climate or cold-climate plants grew around the lakes in past centuries. Cores taken from the ocean bed contain the fossilized shells of ancient sea animals. Such remains often show the temperature of the seawater at the time the animals were alive.

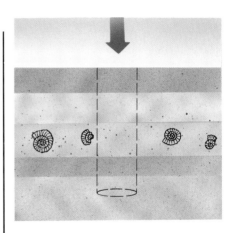

▲ A cylindrical core is obtained by drilling down through layers of sedimentary rocks, formed from mud and sand that were laid down millions of years ago. By studying the fossils and other traces of plant and animal remains found in the rocks, scientists can tell what the climate was like when they were deposited.

The rings seen in the stump of this cedar tree vary in width, showing changes in the amount of rainfall from year to year. ▼

◄ This scene in western India shows present-day climate changes. Because the monsoon rains failed to arrive, sand dunes now cover land where farmers grew crops only four years before this picture was taken.

43

Ice Ages

The evidence

The ice ages of the past left several clues behind. Sedimentary rock is made of layers of sediments deposited in water over millions of years. Some of these layers tell experts that at different times in the past, plants were growing, and other layers show that no plants could grow.

Moving glaciers carved out deep valleys, including the flooded valleys that form the fjords of Norway. The ice scraped grooves on rocks. It also carried down and deposited silt and rocks in shapes called moraines.

At times during the past two billion years, ice has covered large areas of land. We call these times ice ages. We know most about the Ice Age of the Quaternary period — the last 2.5 million years.

Today, about 10% of Earth's land surface is ice-covered. But at various times during the Quaternary period, ice covered from one-fifth to one-half of the land.

The ice cap

Northern Europe, Siberia, and North America had a thick cap of ice and looked like Antarctica does today. In North America, the ice once covered all of Canada and reached as far south as Kansas and Nebraska. At one stage in Europe, the ice covered Denmark and Germany and reached almost to Moscow.

From the southern tip of South America, an ice sheet reached 1,060 miles (1,700 km) north into Argentina and Chile. Another ice sheet capped New Zealand.

During this time, the ice retreated and advanced between 20 and 30 times. Each time this happened, there was a major change of climate. The periods of greatest ice cover are called glacials, and the warmer periods in between are called interglacials.

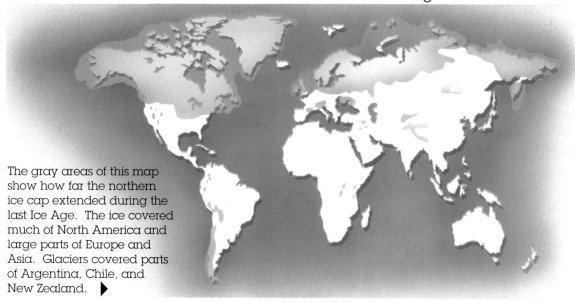

The gray areas of this map show how far the northern ice cap extended during the last Ice Age. The ice covered much of North America and large parts of Europe and Asia. Glaciers covered parts of Argentina, Chile, and New Zealand. ▶

◀ During the last Ice Age, a glacier carved out this valley in northwestern England. Its U shape is typical of valleys formed in this way.

Did You Know?
We are still learning about ancient climates. Newly found traces show that the Earth had six major ice ages before the most recent one, about 2.3 billion, 950 million, 750 million, 650 million, 450 million, and 290 million years ago.

Where we are now

Each glacial lasted between 40,000 and 60,000 years, and the interglacials each lasted between 10,000 and 40,000 years. Scientists think we are now in an interglacial period that began about 10,000 years ago. Europe's climate is now about 9°F (5°C) warmer than it was during a glacial period.

During glacials, so much water was locked up as ice that the ocean level fell between 330 to 460 feet (100-140 m). Dry land appeared between Siberia and Alaska and between the British Isles and Europe.

A present-day Swiss Alpine glacier — a slow-moving river of ice. At its sides and its end, the glacier deposits heaps of stones and dirt, called moraines. Ice melts to form a flowing river. ▼

Climate after the Ice Age

The Fertile Crescent region, from the Mediterranean Sea through the land between the Euphrates and Tigris rivers to the Persian Gulf. Farming in this area began about 10,000 years ago. Our modern wheat comes from the wild wheat that grew in the areas marked. ▶

Carbon-14 dating

One of the greatest tools of the scientists investigating the climate of the past is known as carbon-14 dating.

Some of the atoms of the element carbon are affected by cosmic rays from the Sun and become radioactive carbon-14. All living things absorb carbon, including carbon-14 atoms. After an organism dies, the carbon-14 atoms slowly decay at a constant rate.

Scientists can measure the amount of carbon-14 left, for example, in a piece of timber. From this amount, they can estimate how old the timber is. In this way, carbon-14 atoms act as a calendar reaching back some 50,000 years or more.

The movement and activities of early peoples indicate the climate in which they lived. The earliest people in North America and Australia arrived during the Ice Age. Cave paintings in France and Spain, made near the end of the Ice Age, show that people hunted deer, mammoths, and rhinoceroses in Europe. In North America, hunters left their spear points in the fossil bones of bison, mammoths, and woolly rhinoceroses.

Middle East agriculture developed about 10,000 years ago as the Ice Age ended. As the climate grew warmer, wild wheat began growing in the Fertile Crescent, the western Asian area where some ancient civilizations developed. This wheat could be cultivated.

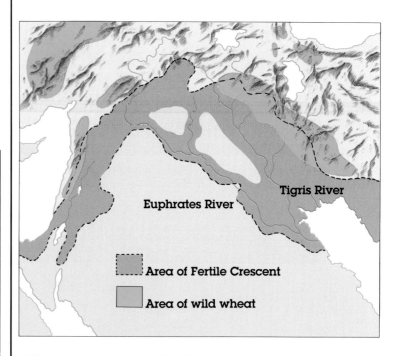

Tigris River

Euphrates River

☐ Area of Fertile Crescent

▨ Area of wild wheat

The warm centuries

About 5,000 years ago, the general climate of the world seems to have been the warmest ever since the end of the Ice Age. In China, subtropical plants and animals like elephants flourished, and bamboo grew farther north than it does today. Early Greeks wore fewer clothes than those of today. Early peoples in North America followed migrating plants and

animals northward into Newfoundland and Labrador. In northern Europe there are a large number of stone circles dating from early times. They were used for astronomical observation, so skies must have been clearer then than today. The peoples living in North America also watched the sky closely. They used natural formations, put marks on cliffs, or built medicine wheels as observatories.

Changes

Some long-term changes took place. The Indus River Valley civilization covered a large area of Pakistan and part of India. Its two chief cities, Harappa and Mohenjo-Daro, were the center of a region where rain fell in large quantities. The Indus Valley people flourished between 2500 BC and 1700 BC, but the rains began to fail. Today, the region is largely dry, with less than 10 inches (25 cm) of rain a year.

In the Americas, a severe climatic change took place from about 1700 BC to 1300 BC. It cooled rapidly in California, the Rocky Mountains, and Central and South America.

▲ The Ring of Brodgar, erected in Orkney, north of Scotland, about 4,500 years ago. The positions of the stones reflect the movement of the Moon, suggesting that the ring was used to watch the night skies.

▲ The remains of the city of Mohenjo-Daro, in the Indus River Valley of Pakistan, lie amid scrub and semidesert. When the city flourished more than 4,000 years ago, the area had plenty of water and fertile farmland.

Climate from the Middle Ages

A warm period began in the Northern Hemisphere in the fourth century AD. South of a line running through the northern coast of the Mediterranean Sea in Europe and the Virginia-North Carolina border in the United States, the weather stayed warm, even growing warmer, for several hundred years.

This warm weather probably helped the growth of the Maya Empire in the Western Hemisphere and led to the drying up of once-good farmland in the Middle East.

Farther north, the climate grew colder again for some time, but was warmer once more by AD 1000, when Norseman Leif Eriksson made his historic voyage to Vinland on the coast of North America.

1

2

3

The frozen Thames

A well-documented guide to European climate in the past is the Thames River in England.

Old London Bridge, across the Thames, had 19 arches on heavy pillars, and it acted like a dam. So when ice did form, it piled up rapidly, and the river was more likely to freeze.

The greatest freeze-up came in the winter of 1683-84, at the height of the Little Ice Age, when the ice was 11 inches (28 cm) thick. A huge Frost Fair was held on the ice, with hundreds of booths. The Thames froze 30 times during the 600 years of Old London Bridge's life. The river has not frozen since the bridge was torn down in 1831.

4

The Little Ice Age

Then the cold returned. The period from about 1450 to 1850 was colder than before or since, and climatologists call it the Little Ice Age.

The start of the Little Ice Age saw the end of Norse settlement in Greenland, begun in the late 900s by Leif's father, Erik the Red. At the time Erik named the island Greenland, it was warm enough to grow food crops.

Glaciers in the mountains of North America and Eurasia grew much larger. At the end of the 1200s, a severe drought forced Indians in southwestern North America to abandon their pueblos and move to wetter areas. As the weather became colder in the late seventeenth century, Scandinavians began to abandon their farms. The middle of the 1800s saw a warming period. But cold weather set in once more in 1879 and brought famine to the people of China and India.

The climate began warming again in the 1920s, although the Baltic Sea froze between Sweden and the Danish island of Sjælland in 1924. During the past hundred years, the climate has been less variable. Most of the changes have been slight or just temporary.

◀◀ Some incidents from the past 2,000 years, showing climatic changes that took place in the Northern Hemisphere:

1. The Maya civilization of North and Central America reached its height between AD 250 and AD 900, at a time of warm climate.

2. When Erik the Red settled in Greenland in about 982, its climate was warm enough for him to call the island green. But in the 1400s, the climate turned colder, and the Norse settlements died out.

3. As the Little Ice Age came on, the weather grew more and more unsettled. In the 1300s, huge storms flooded large areas of low-lying land in northern Europe.

4. The largest of the many Frost Fairs held in London on the Thames River, especially during the Little Ice Age. This picture is based on a painting that was made in 1684.

5. The blight that attacked the potato crop in Ireland in 1846 spread rapidly because the weather had turned very warm and humid.

6. The Baltic Sea froze over during a cold spell in the late 1800s and again in 1924. People could walk across the ice from Sweden to Denmark.

5

6

The Moving Deserts

The yellow areas on this map show the world's deserts as they are today. The darker areas are the regions in danger of turning into deserts. Desertification can result from natural causes, but human activity can also cause it. ▼

Just as the cave paintings in Europe tell us about the climate during the Ice Age on that continent, rock paintings in the Sahara Desert show how the ending of the Ice Age led to the development of the desert.

The paintings were made about 5,500 years ago in the Tassili Mountains of southern Algeria. They show many animals no longer found in the Sahara, including antelope, deer, crocodiles, elephants, and giraffes. One of the most remarkable drawings shows men hunting hippopotamuses from canoes. So the now-dry Sahara was wet at that time.

Grasslands covered much of the Sahara, watered by numerous rivers. Lake Chad was many times its present size, and its water level was about 130 feet (40 m) higher than today.

The Sahara's change from a green and pleasant land to the world's largest desert came when the glaciers of northern Europe were thawing. Rainfall moved farther south, leaving the Sahara region dry.

The Sahara is still moving southward. At its southern edge lies the region known as the Sahel. In this area, the desert gives way to grassland, with scattered trees. The annual rainfall in the Sahel is unpredictable, ranging from about 1.5 to over 6.5 inches (40-170 mm)

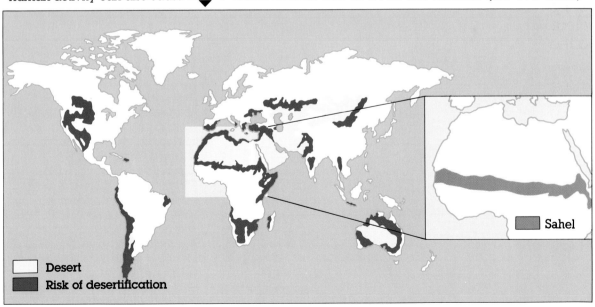

Desert

Risk of desertification

Sahel

in the north of this region. But there is more rainfall in the southern part. The desert moving into the Sahel is one cause of the disastrous series of famines that has taken place in Sudan and Ethiopia in recent years.

There are other large regions in danger of desertification. Prolonged droughts due to changes in rainfall patterns can cause this. But people have made the problem worse by clearing away vegetation and overusing already poor farmland.

▲ One of the rock paintings in the Tassili Mountains in Algeria, showing men tending cattle in an area that is now part of the Sahara. This shows that, in the past, the area must have grown enough vegetation to support cattle grazing.

Did You Know?

The desert sand of the Sahara in Africa sometimes blows over Europe as far as the British Isles. It leaves a fine red dust on cars and other surfaces, and in wet weather produces what is called red rain.

◀ Herding cattle toward green pastures in Niger, in the Sahel. This is one of the areas where unreliable rainfall is causing the Sahara to spread.

6: PEOPLE AND CLIMATE

How People Change Climate

Modern humans, *Homo sapiens sapiens*, have been around for at least 35,000 years.

As we have seen, climate and changes in climate have affected how and where people live. During most of that time, humans have had no effect on climate.

In the past 200 years, things have changed dramatically. In 1800, the world had fewer than one billion people. By the year 2000, the population will reach over six billion.

Polluting the air

The world has become industrialized since 1800. Vast quantities of chemicals and other pollutants are now pumped into the air from factories and other sources. People are now changing the Earth's atmosphere, and in doing this, they are also changing its climate.

One of the earliest changes took place in the climate of large towns. The heat from houses heated by fires made the air around towns warmer. The smoke from those fires hung over the towns like a shroud.

Acid rain facts

Acid rain forms when clouds — and the water they hold — are polluted by chemicals such as nitric acid and sulfuric acid. These chemicals come from factories and car exhausts.

The rain produced by this pollution can fall over 625 miles (1,000 km) or more away from the source. The rain deposits acid on the Earth's surface, poisoning lakes and rivers and damaging buildings, plants, and the soil. The areas most affected are eastern North America, most of Europe, and parts of Asia.

◀ The Dust Bowl in the Great Plains of the United States in the 1930s.

The Dust Bowl

Growing plants unsuited to the climate can result in disaster. In the 1930s, farmers in the Great Plains plowed up the natural prairie grasses that bound the soil together. They planted crops like wheat in a climate suitable mostly for grazing.

They had good crops in wet weather. But in a series of dry summers, wind blew away the surface soil of the land, creating what was called the Dust Bowl. Crops could not grow, livestock died, and thousands of people abandoned their farmland.

◀◀ Opposite: Dead trees in the Black Forest of Germany, shrouded in the acid fog that has killed them.

Smog blankets Mexico City, one of the world's largest cities. It lies high above sea level in a valley that traps pollution from industry and cars. ▼

Smog

Fog combined with smoke has led to heavy outbreaks of smog. Some of the densest smogs occurred in London, Düsseldorf, and Berlin. In these three places, the problem was corrected. But now many other cities, such as Mexico City, Los Angeles, Bangkok, and Cairo, are smog-ridden.

A different kind of climate change results from cutting down trees for lumber or to clear land for farming and buildings. Trees absorb the gas carbon dioxide, which people and animals breathe out, and give out oxygen, which people and animals breathe in. By destroying the forests, the balance of oxygen and carbon dioxide in the atmosphere is changing. Clearing away trees also changes the albedo, or sunlight reflection, of an area.

Forests used to cover about 60% of the world's land. Now they cover less than half that amount. The tropical rain forests are being cut down at the extraordinary rate of 104 acres (42 ha) a minute.

The Greenhouse Effect

Smoke billows from the chimneys of a steel factory in China. The carbon dioxide produced by this kind of heavy industry is one of the main causes of the greenhouse effect that most scientists say is making the Earth grow warmer.

Coal, oil, and natural gas are all fuels that we extract from the ground. Millions of years ago, forest plants decayed and formed coal. Tiny plants and animals in the seas decayed to form oil and natural gas. For this reason, coal, oil, and natural gas are known as the fossil fuels.

When we burn fossil fuels, they give off quantities of the gas carbon dioxide. There has always been a small amount of carbon dioxide in the Earth's atmosphere, but since the start of the Industrial Revolution in the 1700s, the amount has increased. We do not know exactly by how much.

Trapping radiation

Carbon dioxide in the atmosphere allows the Sun's rays and heat to reach the surface of the Earth, but keeps heat from escaping.

Other gases that act the same way are the chlorofluorocarbons (CFCs) that are used in aerosols and refrigerators, and nitrous oxide from burning fossil fuels.

These gases are all called greenhouse gases. This is because they act like the glass of a greenhouse to keep heat inside. Just as the air inside a greenhouse is warmer than the air outside, so the surface of the Earth and the lower layers of our atmosphere both gradually become warmer. This result is called the greenhouse effect.

What are CFCs?

CFCs are compounds of three chemical elements: chlorine, fluorine, and carbon. They are inactive, nonflammable, and colorless, with hardly any odor. They are made under a number of trade names, such as Arcton, Freon, Geon, and Genetron.

They have been used in aerosols and as cooling fluids in air conditioners and refrigerators. When these appliances are scrapped, and when CFC spray cans are used, the CFCs escape into the atmosphere. CFCs are also used to make insulating and packaging foams.

Warming up

There are signs that the Earth is warming up. In some areas, mountain glaciers are growing shorter. The Southern Hemisphere also seems to be getting warmer.

The Earth may be having one of its warmer periods anyway, but most scientists believe that human activity is increasing the greenhouse effect. We must assume that we are responsible for this change so that we will do everything possible to slow down or prevent it before it is too late to do anything.

Greenhouse results

If the greenhouse effect goes on, the world's climates are likely to change greatly. The ice caps will melt, raising the sea level and flooding low-lying coastal areas, drowning many of the world's port cities.

Regions with permanently frozen soil, such as northern Canada and Siberia, may become warm and pleasant places to live.

The rainfall pattern will also change. Some regions will get less rain than they do now, and others will get more. The Sahara might become green again, and other areas might turn into deserts.

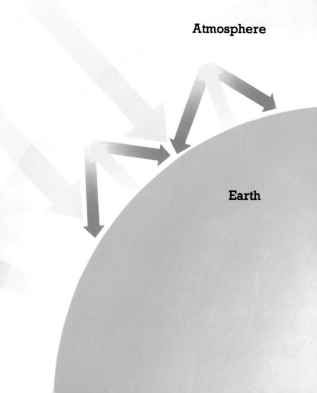

Sun's rays

Atmosphere

Earth

How rays from the Sun penetrate the Earth's atmosphere. Too much carbon dioxide in the air can keep surface heat from radiating back into space, trapping it inside the Earth's atmosphere in the greenhouse effect. Some scientists fear that over the next hundred years, the temperature of the Earth could rise by as much as 9°F (5°C). ▶

The Ozone Layer

The ozone layer of the atmosphere lies between 6 and 30 miles (10-50 km) above the Earth. It protects us from the harmful ultraviolet rays of the Sun.

Ozone, a light blue gas, is another form of oxygen. The molecule of ordinary oxygen is made up of two oxygen atoms. But there are three oxygen atoms in a molecule of ozone. These molecules absorb ultraviolet rays.

You can sometimes detect ozone's sharp odor near electrical machines and in thunderstorms. When ozone is close to the ground, it is harmful to plants, animals, and people. Smog often contains ozone.

The ozone hole over Antarctica. The area of ozone depletion has increased greatly since it was first discovered. The upper diagram shows the hole's area in the early 1980s. The lower picture shows its size in 1989. ▶

The dangers

The Antarctic ozone hole is over an area where there are very few people. If the ozone layer is seriously thinned over other places, these could result:
- More people could develop such things as skin cancers, cataracts, and blindness.
- Some infectious diseases could spread more easily.
- Plants found in plankton could be affected, and this would upset the food chain in the oceans.
- Acid smog might form.
- Food crops, such as rice, might grow in smaller quantities.

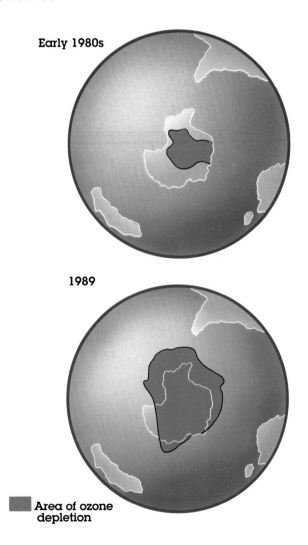

Early 1980s

1989

Area of ozone depletion

Years of tests

British scientists based in Antarctica began measuring the amount of ozone in the ozone layer about 1960. During the early 1980s, they made an unpleasant discovery. Each spring, from September to October, a hole appeared in the layer, right over Antarctica.

Since then, the hole has appeared every spring, growing larger each year. By 1988, it covered all of Antarctica and affected parts of Australia and New Zealand.

Something was attacking the ozone and destroying it. Among the culprits appeared to be the chlorofluorocarbon gases. The ozone hole appeared after CFC gases came into widespread use.

In a 1987 treaty, 24 leading countries agreed to cut the production of CFCs. But by January 1989, the CFCs were attacking the ozone layer over the Arctic and other parts of the world. In 1990, 59 nations agreed to stop making CFCs and other chemicals that can harm the atmosphere.

If the ozone layer is seriously reduced, the Earth's climate may warm up, adding to the greenhouse effect. Unfortunately, CFCs last up to 140 years, so the damage to the ozone layer is likely to be with us for many years.

Aerosol cans

Aerosol cans do not need CFC gases. The United States banned the use of CFCs in aerosol cans in 1978. Some other countries are also acting to ban CFCs. More and more makers are producing spray cans that use other, safer gases. You can check the label to be sure that any aerosol products you use do not contain CFCs or other environmentally harmful chemicals. The safest practice is to use products that come in hand-pumped spray containers.

▲ The British Antarctic Survey Station in western Antarctica, where scientists first detected the hole in the ozone layer.

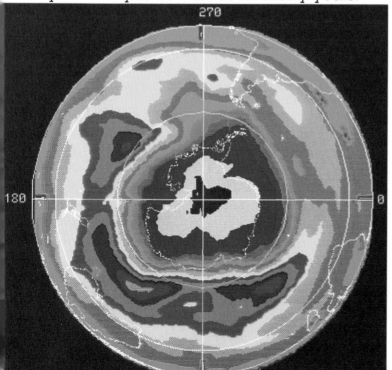

◀ Pictures like this one, taken by the US *Nimbus 7* satellite, help scientists track the ozone hole. It was taken in October 1987, during the Antarctic spring, the time of year when the hole is largest. The greatest depletion of ozone is shown in black. The pink and purple colors show slightly less depleted areas.

Climate in the Future

A rusting, rotting fishing fleet lies ▶
on dry land. A few years ago,
this was the shore of the Aral
Sea, but the water is now
several miles away. Between
1961 and 1989, the Aral Sea
shrank by more than half, from
25,480 square miles (66,000 sq
km) to 14,100 square miles
(36,500 sq km). The water has
become saltier, and most of the
sea's fish have died.

A warm, dry Earth?

If world temperatures go up,
living standards will go down.
Water would be used mainly for
agriculture and essential indus-
tries. People would live in a
grubbier world, rarely washing
clothes, cars, and houses. Less
food could be grown, and prices
would rise. Increased cooling
and freezing needs would cause
shortages of electricity. More
dry forests would burn, followed
by more floods. Melting polar
ice would raise ocean levels
and drown large ports like New
York, Montreal, Los Angeles,
and Tokyo as waters flood
inland for miles.

The world's climate is changing. But it is hard
to see if it is warming up or cooling down. We
may still be in the middle of the interglacial
that began 10,000 years ago, or we may be
nearing another glacial period.

The disastrous droughts and famines that
have gripped Africa have gone on long
enough to indicate that they are part of a
permanent change. Right now, we cannot
tell how much people's activities have
contributed to this change.

The action needed

How will climate changes affect the world's
food supplies? We are accustomed to being
able to grow plenty of food in places like the
plains of North America and Europe.

Now we need to watch the climate to see
whether the traditional "granaries of the
world" will remain able to supply enough food
for the hungry billions of the coming years.
The study of past climates can help us to see
what future climates may be like.

But in working to safeguard food crops in

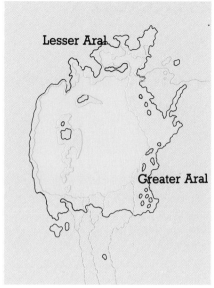

▲ The Aral Sea as it was in 1961, outlined in black, and in 1989, colored blue, when its islands had grown much larger and it had split into two seas.

one area, we must be careful not to upset the climate or the environment in another. The Soviets have already run into trouble by drawing water from the rivers that flow into the Aral and Caspian seas in order to supply industry and farmland.

As a result, the Aral Sea is fast drying up, leaving vast areas of useless wasteland. The level of the Caspian Sea has also dropped alarmingly. Because less fresh water flows into the Caspian, it is becoming too salty, harming its fish and other life.

To correct this, the Soviets are planning to take water from the major rivers, such as the Ob and the Yenisey, that flow into the Arctic Ocean. But without this fresh river water, ice might not form on the Arctic Ocean.

If that happened, the climate of the whole area might become up to 18°F (10°C) warmer. This might cause a northward shift of the winds that now bring rain to Europe and central Asia, leading to drought. Planners must think several steps ahead when tampering with the Earth's climate.

▲ Relief workers in Mali provide a porridge of soybeans, sorghum syrup, and oil for starving women and children. Drought is causing famines in large areas of Africa.

59

Glossary

Albedo: The amount of light that a surface reflects.

Altitude: The height of a place above sea level.

Anticyclone: An area of high pressure where winds blow in a spiral outward from the center.

Asteroid: One of about 30,000 bodies that orbit the Sun midway between Mars and Jupiter.

Atom: The smallest amount of an element. Each element is made up of identical atoms that are different from the atoms of all other elements.

Axis: A line about which something rotates. The Earth rotates around an axis running through it from the North to the South Pole.

Carbon dioxide: A colorless, odorless gas that is breathed out by animals and absorbed by plants.

Carbon-14 dating: A way to find out an object's age from the amount of carbon-14 it contains.

Chlorofluorocarbons (CFCs): Gases made up from chlorine, fluorine, and carbon. These gases damage the ozone layer.

Condense: To change from a gas or vapor to a liquid or solid.

Contour lines: Lines on a map that join together points of equal height.

Cosmic rays: Streams of high-speed, electrically charged subatomic particles present in space.

Crystals: Pieces of solid substances that have regular shapes, as found in salt or snowflakes.

Cyclone: An area of low pressure where winds blow in a spiral inward toward the center.

Data: A group of facts, measurements, or observations.

Dense: The condition of something that is heavy in proportion to its size.

Depression: Another name for a cyclone.

Desertification: The process in which land changes from a fertile condition to desert.

Evaporation: The change from a liquid or a solid to a vapor or gas.

Food chain: A series of plants and animals, each feeding on another in the chain.

Fossil fuels: Coal, oil, and natural gas. These fuels formed from ancient plants and animals.

Front: The boundary between two air masses that have different temperatures.

Genetically: Relating to genes, the tiny units that determine what traits plants, animals, and humans inherit from their parents.

Glacial: A period when large areas of land were covered by ice.

Helium: A very light, colorless, nonflammable gas. It is often used to float balloons.

Hemisphere: Half a globe. The Earth is divided into Northern and Southern hemispheres.

High: A short term for an area of high pressure; an anticyclone.

Himalayas: A huge mountain chain north of India. It contains the world's highest peaks.

Humidity: The amount of water vapor in the air.

Hurricane: A tropical cyclone that produces a violent storm.

Hydrogen: The lightest chemical element. It normally exists as a gas.

Ice Age: The period when large areas of land were covered by ice during the Pleistocene epoch of the Quaternary period, between one million and 10,000 years ago. Other ice ages occurred much earlier in Earth's history.

Ice caps: Sheets of ice covering large areas of land, as in Antarctica and Greenland.

Industrial Revolution: The development of machines and factories that replaced handcrafted goods in Britain, Europe, and the United States during the eighteenth and nineteenth centuries.

Interglacial: A warm period between glacials, during which the glaciers melted back.

Isobars: Lines connecting points of equal pressure.

Landmass: A very large area of land, often a continent.

Latitudes: Regions lying north or south of the equator, marked on maps by imaginary lines. The higher the latitude, the farther north or south it is from the equator.

Lichen: An organism consisting of a fungus and an alga living together. Lichen grows as colored patches on rocks, trees, or soil.

Low: A short term for an area of low pressure, or cyclone.

Magnetic field: The area of force surrounding a magnet. A magnetic field surrounds Earth, but is weakest at the poles.

Mercury: A silver-colored metal that is a liquid at normal temperatures. It is often used in thermometers and barometers.

Meteorite: A lump of metallic or rocky material from outer space that lands on the Earth.

Middle Ages: The period of European history between ancient and modern times, from about AD 500 to 1500.

Molecule: A unit of matter containing two or more atoms. The atoms can be from the same element or from different elements.

Monsoon: A wind that changes direction according to the season. Monsoons usually bring heavy rain to certain parts of the world in summer.

Nitrous oxide: A colorless, odorless gas, used in aerosol cans.

Occluded: A term describing a front that lies between two cold air masses.

Ozone: A form of oxygen whose molecules consist of three oxygen atoms instead of the usual two.

Pigment: A substance that gives a plant or animal its color.

Plankton: Tiny plants and animals that drift in the ocean's upper layer of water and that form the main food of some animals, such as whales.

Pollen: A fine, powdery substance produced by flowering or cone-bearing plants. Pollen helps the plant produce seeds.

Precipitation: A general term for the different forms of rain, hail, sleet, and snow.

Prevailing wind: A more or less continual wind blowing from mainly one direction in a particular region.

Quaternary period: The most recent period of Earth's history, beginning about 2.5 million years ago. It includes the Pleistocene epoch.

Radar: A device that bounces radio waves off an object in order to measure the distance to it and track its movements.

Radiation: The flow of particles and rays, such as light and radio waves. It is also the energy released from an atom.

Radiation balance: The heating effect of the Sun on the Earth, after measuring the heat from the Sun and the amount of this heat that is lost from the Earth.

Radioactive: Giving off nuclear energy. Radioactivity can be harmful or harmless and long-lived or short-lived, depending on which element is radioactive.

Sedimentary rock: Rock, such as sandstone, that was formed by deposits of tiny particles from other rock.

Solar flare: A powerful eruption from the surface of the Sun.

Solar wind: The flow of electrically charged particles, or cosmic rays, from the Sun.

Sulfur dioxide: A colorless, poisonous gas, produced from rotting plant or animal matter, or by volcanoes.

Sunspots: Periodic dark areas that appear on the surface of the Sun, showing increased activity inside the Sun.

Temperate: Having a climate between polar and tropical. On a map, the temperate zones lie between 23.5° and 60° north and south of the equator.

Tropics: A zone around the Earth on either side of the equator, where the climate is warm or hot all year round.

Vacuum: A space entirely empty of anything, including air. Other matter will always try to enter a vacuum.

Vapor: Particles of moisture or solids forming clouds or smoke. Air can hold a certain amount of moisture that is not visible.

Index

A **boldface** number shows that the entry is illustrated on that page. The same page often has text about the entry, too.